God and Other Monsters

STORIES & POEMS
RAPHAEL MATTO

Visit www.raphaelmatto.com/books to download free versions of this book
in a variety of electronic formats (Kindle, Nook, Sony, ePub, PDF) or to order print copies

ALSO BY RAPHAEL MATTO

Mars
100 bad poems

God and Other Monsters

Brooklyn, New York

Designed and produced by Raphael Matto LTD

Typeset in Whitman

When Kent Lew created Whitman in 2002 he was inspired by classic 20th-century text faces like Caledonia,
Electra, and Joanna. "I think of the typeface as having an essentially American quality. I hesitate
to bring that up nowadays, because of our society's current nationalistic fervor."

Electra LT Std

Designed in 1935 by William Addison Dwiggins, Electra has been a standard book typeface since its release.
"If you don't get your type warm it will be just a smooth, commonplace, third-rate piece of good machine
technique, no use at all for setting down warm human ideas, just a box full of rivets."

and Joanna MT Std

The Joanna typeface was designed by Eric Gill in 1930-1931, based on type originally cut by Robert Granjon
(1513–1589). Gill created the typeface for his printing firm Hague & Gill – which he formed to
give his idle son-in-law an occupation – and named the typeface after his daughter.

Fourth edition, September 2014

Library of Congress Cataloging-in-Publication Data:
    Matto, Raphael, 1979
    God and Other Monsters: Stories and Poems by Raphael Matto—1st American ed.
    ISBN-13: 978-1501002946 (CreateSpace-Assigned)
    ISBN-10: 1501002945
    BISAC: Poetry / American / General

Acknowledgements

I would like to thank my writing teachers for their guidance and encouragement: Mary Ruefle, Leslie Ullman, Jody Gladding—the following readers for their friendship and generosity: Lillian Kwok, Sophfronia Scott, Baaron Schulte—Pandapanther for being flexible with my work schedule—Art Farm Nebraska & Ed Dadey—George Kokkinidis for design advice—and also Glen Sharah and Lee Sentes who helped me out in a pinch.

The table

For Mom, Dad, and Byron

God

and Other

Monsters

W E'RE TOLD NOT TO TOUCH GODS, but there seem to be
so many this season. Above us, huge, three eat clouds and moan—
below, a tiny family of them runs in a line
toward someone who is afraid.

The hardest monster to be

THE GIRL KNEW she was a monster—just not what kind. Some nights she flapped out her window as a bat (vampire), leaving her parents snoring and oblivious. Other nights she practiced staggering across the grassy fields behind the cow paddock (zombie)—or hunted down foxes on all fours (werewolf). But it never felt right. It was always too *easy*.

She could do it all: kill without remorse, raise the dead (she'd tried it on her cat, Socks, and her mother, Sarah)—she could fly, turn boys into stone, turn boys into gold, turn boys into girls—that one never got old. She could hear other people's wishes, run across the surface of a lake, hold her breath long enough to explore neighboring galaxies. She had retractable fangs, claws, horns, wings, several types of tails, could control the trajectory of lightening with her facial expressions, slow down and almost stop time.

When she was feeling gloomy, she would disperse—let her bosons blow out over the plains, mixing into the stratosphere where a warm omnipresent tingling lightened her spirit. The only thing she couldn't do was find a boyfriend. Or … maybe that wasn't quite right. She just needed a good friend. Maybe, like, two really good friends—they could be a triumvirate or something. They could help her figure out what the heck kind of monster she was.

◆

She watched SO much TV.

It had served as her catalogue; each new monster show gave her something to try out—but lately it felt like a dead end. One day, when she was explaining this all in a hypothetical roundabout way to her father, he said: "You know, they haven't thought of everything."

She didn't understand.

"Well, there are monsters people haven't discovered yet, can't even imagine, monsters folks just plain forgot about. Not everything is on TV, kiddo. Try making up something yourself."

"I can't do that!"

"Wanna bet? Have a little faith."

That night she stood under the stars, shivering a little in her pajamas, and began imagining a world she'd never seen. Fear crept up beside her. What if she couldn't do it? But even as she fretted, mountains curled from a boiling void— phantoms shrieked among the crags, flinging their bodies up at her, falling back on a viscous ocean that heaved—the unevolved embryos of boyfriends, best friends, millions of them foamed the protoplasm, clawing for life, crying out for her love. She sobbed, suddenly sure that she did love them. *She loved them so much.* But she couldn't hold it all together. She had to let go, and as she collapsed the successive concussive detonations of her mind annihilated utterly everything … until she was lying in her back yard, alone again, gasping.

She tried again. And again, for almost six hours, until it was done; finally she let herself rest. *Now this is hard,* she thought to herself. *This is the kind of monster I want to be.*

~ *August, 2012*

Horses, backwards

You've got to spin the television
if you want the pictures to move

Spin it like a globe spin it
backwards so the horses

all run backwards and the cowboy
fires a bullet from his lung

right through his shirt
into the muzzle

of a six shooter

That's nothing

An Indian does the same trick blindfolded

and his brother
springs up and fires from his forehead
into the gun behind him

On another channel

a woman opens her legs
and ingests a child

Deep in her body its DNA is ripped apart
everyone

is murdered

like this

Lions
give birth
to antelope

chewing them together
appraising

their first awkward steps
back

into the world

Astronauts find
an American flag
on the moon

They bring it home

it looks brand new

inspiring workers

to unscrew skyscrapers
and plant
hundred year old trees

by the thousands

and jackhammer the roads

so the horses can all run backwards
in our beautiful fields

~ April, 2014

Orphans

THE CHILDREN AT THE ORPHANAGE were beautiful. One had a lazy eye, and when he trotted across the playground his hair, neatly parted down the middle, flopped up and down as if his mind were throwing itself into the sky again and again.

My new wife and I agreed that he should be our son—I had adopted Jill that morning, but we were already getting along so well—and approached the boy, whose name was Jimmy.

"You don't have a mother? No father?" I asked.

"No. I'm a orphan, which is why I live in this sad place with the others."

"How would you like to come home with us, Jimmy?" Jill said, smiling. "I'll be your mother. Jack says there's a big swimming pool."

"Do you have a cat?"

"No, Jimmy, sorry. I don't," I admitted.

"That's okay."

I tossed Jimmy's luggage into the trunk and we all piled into the car. My wife got out the list.

"Should we cross off these other orphanages or keep going?" She asked. "Saint Mary's Sisters is out in Litchfield county—it would be a wonderful drive up the river. Oh—I want to keep going!"

I turned to Jimmy in the back seat, "Whattaya say, bucko? Wanna visit another orphanage on the way home?"

"You're going to take me to another orphanage?"

The look on his face was priceless and I had to laugh. "No no, you're part of the family now. It's just ... well, someone else might want to be part of our family too."

"Okay." Jimmy still seemed nervous, but I didn't want to upset Jill, so I smiled reassuringly at the rear view mirror and pulled out onto Route 1 heading north.

That part of the countryside was covered with orphanages. Some were run down; old matchstick barns like parallelograms, orphans standing in their fields next to cows—poor souls with no parents, or no children, or no best friend, or no pets. I felt suddenly glad that I'd renovated my house the previous fall; it had seemed big and empty when I left that morning, but now I imagined Jimmy running around, filling up the spaces with his toys and friends—Jill reading her books by the old stone fireplace—and maybe even a new sister putting her makeup on in the hallway. A sense of calm anticipation settled over me as we drove into Saint Mary's.

The director interviewed Jill, Jimmy, and me, then called over a young woman—about seventeen years old—watching TV in the common room.

None of us liked Amy at first. She was bossy: "*No one* is allowed on my side of the room, got it? I need *privacy*." Amy had moved into the orphanage the previous year. "Some of the girls here—they never had a brother. Some never had a sister. Well boo hoo. *I never had either.*" But there was something irresistible about Amy—maybe it was her club foot, or bad breath, or her self importance—I even felt a bit of sibling rivalry brewing between us—so I chose her—and it felt wonderful to finally have a sister. I threw Amy's bags on top of Jimmy's.

The Roma was next on the list, an orphanage that catered to elderly orphans who didn't have grandchildren. We picked out a man who seemed like he'd be a nice grandfather for Jimmy, gave him a key and directions to our house, and told him to settle into the little apartment above the attached garage.

"Okay, we have time for one more orphanage," I said. There was still an empty seat in the back between Jimmy and Amy (Amy was technically Jimmy's aunt, I realized, feeling more and more satisfied). "Who wants what? Does everyone have an uncle? There's an uncle orphanage just down the highway here. No? Everyone has an uncle?"

Amy was pouting—we hadn't stopped at McDonald's like she'd wanted to; she and I had fought for half an hour about it.

Jill seemed lost in thought.

"What is it, sweetie?" I asked.

"Well, you know, it just crossed my mind—and I was so happy when you picked me up at the orphanage this morning, really—I had been there for so long, ever since my Darryl died—but I was thinking, if it was alright with you, that we could stop at The Amant. All those years with Darryl I never had a lover. Maybe I might pick one out? It would mean so much to me."

"I'm not sure that's a good idea, Jill. That would make me—"

"A cuckold?" Amy offered, helpfully.

"I just don't know how I feel about it, Jill. You're my wife now."

Jill did not look happy. She said something under her breath.

"What's that, Jill?" I was getting angry.

She was too. "I said: then I'm *still* an orphan!" She started crying. "I don't want to be one of those old woman who's never had an affair."

I glanced over at Amy for help. "Hey—you picked her," she scoffed. "No Micky D's, no sympathies. You are on your own."

"I'd like to stop and get a cat," Jimmy said after a while.

~ March, 2014

8

God of robots

For Freja

FREJA, I am here
to spank you
you can
adjust the pressure with this dial

Little girls like fields and

you are a little
fire
picnicking in the dry

meadow

I will crush you with my godhood

all your wildflowers blown out
Then I will do my own thing

malfunctioning
for a while

I made you full of blood so delicate you will die

little heart
tied up with veins like a fly
I can almost
see

the pin
bleeding

I want to kiss you with my metal
but you spread your death all over the ground

instead of getting old

with me

*

I pull another girl
by her dress out of a school bus
window, screaming

but she will never be you

~ March, 2014

The business lover

O<small>N THE SUBWAY</small> she decides to quit her job. By the time she gets home she feels free. She takes off the stiff black suit and washes her makeup down the drain.

She jumps on her boyfriend's back and rides him around and lies to him—she tells him she already quit. He pats her head and tells her baby you'll be okay you can go back to school and he strips her clothes off and makes popcorn and lollipops her and covers her with pajamas and they watch Star Wars and she tries to dream of some other career but it's hopeless it's so totally hopeless it's something about Darth Vader. Just staring at her. Breathing through the speakers.

His whole black head in her hands.

Her boyfriend on the couch—she looks over at him—is like a huge puppy giraffe, its bony legs crowding her, sucking its thumb, the same boy it was at eleven, nodding off. She looks down at Vader—between her legs, breathing into her.

It's a trap.

It's the part where the rebels are losing, their ships exploding out in space, Solo and Leia captive on the forest moon—the Emperor is killing Luke with electricity and it feels ... *really good*—the electricity—on her teeth, under her pajamas, under her skin. Deep in her the rebels are dying and it feels *so* good.

Vadar climbs on top of her, his mechanical legs heavy. She unscrews his breastplate with her fingernails, pulls out his blue wires, his green wires, slips off his leather gloves, touches him; parts that are metal, parts that are plastic, parts that are flesh, scarred—he groans, his breathing becomes erratic, she takes his light saber with both hands. It discharges and recoils, the red beam surprisingly heavy, she can smell it burning the air, she can hear the blade buzz. She could kill Darth Vadar.

He enters her world.

The light saber rolls across the floor. "Who are you?" she asks, gasping, gazing up at him, her fingers crackling on his back.

"I am your—fmphth," (she covers his mouth as she comes). "I am your—mguthfr," (she covers his mouth again and holds her hand there). When it's finally over she lifts off his helmet.

In the morning she puts on the black suit, rising quickly up the elevator shaft.

~ May, 2014

Dreams do not exist, according to mice

SCIENTISTS DISCOVERED THAT dreams do not exist. We've all just been imagining them, they said.

"Isn't imagining a dream the same as having one?" Someone asked.

We learned that, apparently, no—it's a little bit different.

"Can you prove it?"

Yes, the scientists said, but they would need some mice.

"How many mice do you need?"

Way, way too many mice, as it turned out.

~ September, 2013

We built Him

AWARE OF OUR OWN deeper needs, we built Him. Advanced hydraulics and propulsion technologies finally made it possible and after years of fundraising and debate we broke ground.

Our scholars had found a god at the center of every culture except for ours. That explained why so many of us felt unfulfilled, they argued; without a god, who would look after our souls? The philosophers stroked their beards—even if we were able to create a god, would it be too deliberately planned? Why hadn't a god arisen naturally? Who would truly believe in a *made* god?

It would work, though, in the end. A mountain was selected—His features were sculpted into it with dynamite, our artists working at a distance while their apprentices distributed and synchronized the blasts. Gradually, behind the dust-cloud of debris, we recognized His shape. He was us, looked like us, and gazed down benevolently—round shoulders lost in the clouds. We all breathed a sigh of relief to look upon Him.

The base of the mountain was cleared away with more dynamite and carefully replaced by a latticework platform of steel. This was where he stood and for many years we lived in His shadow. We loved Him. We sang to Him. Houses crowded the grassy slope by His feet. But eventually the day came—we'd gathered enough fuel. Hundreds of rockets were bolted to a belt around His waist and, on a cool winter morning, the countdown began. Many cried, while others— those who had contributed to His production—waited in silence, praying that He would not be damaged. But the engines fired smoothly in sequence, exerting the steady, monstrous force required to lift Him gently off of Earth and into the sky, then carried him quickly away from us, disappearing altogether into the glare of heaven.

He watches over us in solemn orbit. We look for Him at night, amongst the stars—His deposits of quarts reflect bits of sunlight like signals in code. Some say He will return one day, pulled down by gravity, ringed again by fire—that He will bring his final judgements with Him.

~ August, 2013

I couldn't stop writing books

I WANTED SOMETHING to read, so I wrote a book. It took an enormous effort,but the book was wonderful—everyone said so. I wrote another book and placed it on top of the first. The little stack looked nice, so I called in sick and sat down to write another one. Then another. I wrote books about aging, lizards, Yoga, and the differences between cats and rabbits. It got easy, like surfing the internet, like buying stuff—I couldn't stop. I built a bookshelf and wrote twenty books a day until I filled it up. Some of the books I wrote were best sellers, some were un-loved, undiscovered, and some I never published. My editor invited me to a party, but I had books to write—and I had to move to a larger apartment because mine was full of my books. A few weeks later, when I was writing almost a hundred books a day, I bought a library to store my books and set a librarian to work organizing them; they overflowed on the library tables faster than she could organize them. I wrote a book about every person on the planet, every person who had died. It was easy to imagine them all. I wrote so many books no one knew what to read anymore. Everyone had one or more of my books. I began to wonder if books weren't so important after all, and sometimes I wished there would be an end.

~ *September, 2013*

A YOUNG INVENTOR BUILT a small town in his bedroom. First he made a sun, then air, and then a forest. When these were all working well and the town seemed a pleasant place to live, he built cats and dogs, set them loose, glued together some houses from model kit parts, and with great care made a fair maiden. He wound her up and she began singing and picking apples from a tree he had screwed onto the corner of her back yard.

The town needed a witch, the inventor decided—like all good fairy tales. He thumbed a gruesome face out of putty and stuck a rusty computer chip to the back of her head. Then he gave her a shock from a battery and buried her in the graveyard. Hopefully she would misdirect her revenge onto the townsfolk.

The inventor also assembled a small bicycle for the maiden to ride around on, until he had time to put together a horse. Then he went to sleep.

◆

When the inventor got home the next day and checked on his town, the maiden was curled up on her bed crying. The bike lay discarded on the front lawn. *Maybe she's bored*, the inventor thought. Since he had no way of asking what was wrong, he built a father. Parts were getting scarce; he used a pencil stub as a peg leg and cut hands out of felt. He sat the father on the maiden's bed and leaned in close to hear their conversation.

"Are you lonely, Daughter?" The father asked in a tiny voice, patting her back with his soft hands. "Is that what's wrong?"

"No, father. I can't ... it's too embarrassing ... I'm bleeding, father."

The inventor quickly put together a mother. He used Legos for her feet—she would have trouble fetching water—a Campbell's soup label for her dress, and a doll's head. But he tied on a strong cloth apron, gave her a beautiful wooden brush, and set her down on the bed, brushing the girl's hair. Then he turned in for the night.

◆

The next morning the inventor discovered that the witch had finally dragged herself out of the graveyard. Or maybe one of the dogs had dug her up. He looked through a magnifying glass and found footsteps leading into the forest, but it was too dark in the forest to see clearly, even when he aimed his penlight between the branches.

He decided to watch the maiden at her chores. She scrubbed floorboards on her knees, cleaned soot from the chimney, and hung sheets on the line; when the inventor turned on his table fan they both watched the sheets lift. A little later the maiden dropped her dress to shower in the shed; the inventor blushed and looked away. *Maybe I should warn her*, he thought. He wrote "BEWARE OF WITCH" on a small note and pinned it to the clothes line.

Later that night, as the inventor paused in the doorway to his room, he heard the mother exclaim, "There is no witch! This note is a joke—a boy fancies you, that's all. Rascal boys will sniff you out now that you are a woman."

◆

That night the inventor couldn't sleep. He thought about the maiden pushing her broom, her faraway voice. He rolled over and looked at his town. Moonlight from his window illuminated the tree; a few apples littered the ground and then the leaves rustled.

"Hey," he whispered.

After a moment, the witch dropped down the trunk and crouched half-hidden in the grass. The apple in her mouth glittered as she peered at the sky; a basket under her right arm bulged with more apples. The witch had attached cats to her legs that hissed and arched their backs when the inventor inspected them. She had also connected what looked like a SIM card to the computer chip on her head. *That must be why my cellphone stopped working*, the inventor thought. The witch reached into her basket and pulled out an apple. She held it up into the air.

Is she offering it to me? The inventor wondered. He looked into the witch's eye sockets as they searched the sky. *How does she know I'm here?* He hesitated, then reached down and, when he picked the tiny apple from her hand, she shrank away. The inventor looked at the apple under his bedside lamp. It was the size of a blueberry. *Why haven't I tried the apples before?* He asked himself. He put it in his mouth and it melted like candy. *Delicious.* When he looked back at the apple tree, the witch was gone.

The inventor picked several more apples off the lawn and ate them, beginning to feel the pull of sleep, the suddenly strong pull of sleep. It was only then—too late—that he noticed another apple carefully arranged inside a bed of tiny leaves, gleaming in the moonlight on the fair maiden's windowsill.

~ November, 2011

The god of whales

THIS BLACK god
   is resting in our sheep paddock.
      She dragged five dead sailors up the lane, tangled
in harpoons and rope, a skiff
splintered in the forest behind them.

Sheep slip off
when they try to climb Her, but my wife
makes it up barefoot.

"I can see everything—
all the way to Frank's barn!"

At lunchtime an eerie roll of whalesong
thrills the rookery
and the wide shadow of flukes
passes over us like a hand.

~ July 2012

The woman who gave birth to a ghost

AFTER SHE SCREAMED it out in the ER they could hear it wailing—so it was healthy—but no one could see the thing. A nurse got her hands on it, threw a little sheet over it and wrestled it into a crib. It wanted its mother, but when it fed, it drained her in ways she couldn't describe.

~ July, 2012

Bill and Mabel

MABEL SAT DOWN for dinner in a cold suburban house with two TVs. She clawed hair out of her eyes, and dug in. Bill sat at the opposite end of the table, picking at his teeth.

"We should go on a road trip."

"You don't know how to drive," Mabel said, spitting a chewed toe into the blood on her plate.

"There's no more fatties to eat in this town—the little mean ones taste, like, awful. Lets go to Graceland."

"Graceland is more about Elvis than Paul Simon, you wouldn't like it."

Bill rolled his enormous eye. "I mean for the fatties."

So they went to Graceland. Graccland, Memphis Tennessee—they went to Graceland.

"I thought America was full of fatties. Last week was good but all I see today is that skinny guy on roller-skates."

"Get him!"

"I already tried. It's just frustrating."

They sat on a bench and watched the guy skate around and taunt them.

"Do you ever wonder if they have feelings? Like us, I mean."

"No, but you should stop calling them fatties. It's not their fault they have to eat hamburgers. What if someone called you a spaz, spaz?"

"I'm not a spaz!!!"

"Uh huh."

"Whatever. Lets get out of here, it's too hot. The big ones are all hiding now anyway."

They walked north along the interstate kicking cars into lake Michigan.

"What do we do with all their stuff?"

"I don't know. Just unplug everything—remember to turn off the lights and shit like that."

"Sometimes I feel like an intelligent power is watching over us, judging our way of life."

Bill stopped and looked at Mabel standing in the road. "If something is watching, it's cheering for us all the way—a big fan."

~ *October, 2009*

Billy's last ice cream cone

"Dinner!"

"Shouldn't we wait for Grampa?"

"He probably died in a field," Gramma said. "Lets eat."

"He went upstairs with the newspaper a few hours ago," Dad said. "Go check on him if you'd like."

Billy tossed his napkin on the table and scrambled out of his chair, then up the stairs.

"You shouldn't have brought that *innocent* child into this world," Gramma said, shaking her head. "It was selfish."

"There's room for one more little boy, Mother," Mom said.

"We can always kill him if money gets tight," Dad offered.

"Is that what you're worried about, Mother?" Mom took Gramma's hand across the table. "That we'd kill you first?"

"Nonsense," Gramma said, pulling her hand away and smoothing her napkin on her lap. "But you *would* kill me first—of course you would. Look at his plate, you gave him extra potatoes and he's half my size."

"Oh, Mother. Don't you remember when I was a little girl? How much you loved me?"

"Of course not."

"Grampa's dead!" Billy called down from the second floor. "He died in the bathtub!"

"Drain the water and come back to the table!" Mom yelled.

When Billy was seated again, they began eating.

"I wish Grampa hadn't died," Billy said. "He always gives me his pudding."

"Well, now we can *all* share the extra pudding," Gramma said.

"Can I have your pudding?"

"No."

"Don't ask to share food, Billy," Dad said, glancing at Gramma.

Billy hung his head. "Grampa always dies before dinner."

"That's because he doesn't eat enough for Breakfast," Mom said. "You know what I always say."

"Breakfast is important," Billy mumbled, pushing away the eggplant on his plate.

"That's right, Billy," Gramma said. "Eat it all!" She forked the eggplant on Billy's plate, bulging her eyes at him.

"Did anything happen today?" Mom asked. "Anything out in the world that might have upset him?"

Dad cleared his throat. "Well the Rex Sox lost again, if that's what you're getting at."

Mom snapped her fingers. "That's it. He must have seen it in the paper."

"What does it feel like when you die, Gramma?" Billy asked.

"You'll know soon enough," Gramma said.

"It's like sleeping," Mom said.

"That's not true." Gramma said, then turned to Billy, smiling. "Do you really want to know?"

Billy nodded.

Gramma looked at Mom. Mom frowned, then shrugged. "Go ahead. He's old enough."

"Well. First there's pain—oh, it does hurt," Gramma said, wrinkling her nose. "Maybe a funny feeling in your hand, and suddenly you can't breathe. Or maybe it's a stroke and the pain is in your head. Maybe someone stabs you in the heart!" Gramma jabbed her knife at Billy's chest.

"Ouch! You're hurting me," Billy said, giggling.

"Mother."

Gramma turned her knife on the butter block and slapped a large chunk onto her potatoes. "After the pain is gone, you only have yourself for company. And a comfortable chair to sit on."

"I never got a chair," Dad said.

"You have to look around for it," Mom said.

After dinner, Mother and Father washed dishes while Billy played chess with Grampa. Grandma read a book in the living room, snacking on cashews.

"Your father is doing his part," Dad whispered. It's your mother—she's just … always alive, sitting there at every meal. The bank won't give us another loan. And I'm working so hard down at the factory."

"I know you are, honey."

"It's not enough. I could die for a while—I'm a big guy, I eat a lot too—but if I miss any more days they'll give my job to one of the guys on the dock."

"What about the Union?"

"The Union can't do anything if I'm dead."

"Well, what if I die for a little while?" Mom said.

"No, I need you. It has to be your mother. Or Billy."

"Stop it. You know how hard it is for little kids when they die. All his friends will grow up, die. They'll be like strangers to him."

"Okay, so it's got to be your mother. How do we do it?"

"I don't know," Mom said, scrubbing hard at the frying pan. "We have to think of something sort of … permanent."

"Kill her forever?"

"No, that's impossible—she'll find a way out of anything. But maybe if we … I don't know, cut off her head—we'd get a few years of peace and quiet. We could save a little money, maybe Grampa would even eat with us at Christmas."

"What do we tell her when she comes back? It might be awkward."

"That's why we make it look like an accident."

"What are you two love birds whispering about?" Grampa said, limping into the kitchen. "Sorry—I'm still a little stiff. I hope everything is okay."

"Everything is fine, Dad. We were just talking about mother. Where is she anyway?"

"She took Billy out in the car. Said they were going to go share a really big ice cream cone."

~ November, 2013

The god of toys

T HIS YELLOW god was digging through the battery box for AAAs when our cat Mittens sniffed her out; she's dying in our kitchen sink now (Frank Jr. heard Mittens drag her across his xylophone and is still standing here crying up at me).

She pulled her own spine out through the top and held it up like a sword to fend me off. I put it on the counter where it rolled back and forth like a nail, tried fresh AAAs—they didn't work—then carefully took her body apart, working legs out of sockets, gingerly removing a tiny shimmering vest, belt, and pewter toolkit. I brushed out her hair—she must have been climbing in the walls, or a rat's nest—rubbed her face clean with my thumb, then ran her parts under the faucet for a while before putting her back together.

She's staring at me now but I don't know what else to do. All I can think of is Frank's goldfish who died the same way—so colorful and angry, motionless in bottom of the sink—and how Frank's mother cut her hand the last time she was here, and we all stood around waiting for the bleeding to stop, so she could leave.

~ July, 2012

"Die! Die! Die!"

Our baby's first sentence.

~ July, 2012

Bill and Mabel land on Mars

"So this is Mars," Bill said, morose. "You tricked me."

"Don't feel bad. There's stuff to do here."

They ate spaceships, then sucked on the jelly of alien livestock.

"Do you know what a 'wife' is?" Mabel asked.

"No ... why?" Fuel was exploding in Bill's stomach; his eyes watered.

"I heard a guy scream 'She's my wife' once. 'She's my wife—don't kill her.' It just made me want a wife ... you know, the way he said it."

Bill gestured at the vast infinity of space, losing interest. "We could go anywhere, do anything." They knew how to jog the black vacuum.

"I think you're my wife," Mabel said, then showed all her beautiful teeth.

~ July, 2011

Her disappearing hand

ONE NIGHT she told me that her hand disappeared when I wasn't looking at it.

"Does it hurt?" I asked, not sure if she was joking.

"No," she replied, not sure if I was joking.

It was hard to believe, since I had no evidence that her hand *actually* disappeared when I wasn't looking at it.

"I'm telling you, it disappears! And it's not just my hand."

"But I can't stay awake and watch you all night," I said. "How about this: I'll wait until you fall asleep before I close my eyes."

"Okay," she said and lay down—but then turned to me, frightened. "What if *you* disappear when I close *my* eyes?"

I assured her. "I don't disappear. I don't. Really." It was true.

"This isn't fair," She said. "Why is this happening to me?"

"I don't know. Maybe you stopped being real," I guessed. "And now I'm just imagining you."

"Why did that happen?"

"How should I know."

She looked miserable, tears balled in her eyes.

"Alright, lets retrace your steps," I said. "When was the first time you disappeared?"

She sniffed and thought for a while. "In the afternoon, when we brought in the groceries. When you went out to get the mail, remember? The grocery bag I was carrying was on the floor when you got back—the melon was smashed, and the eggs. The bag must have fallen out of my hands because I disappeared when you left."

"Okay, what happened right before that."

"I killed myself in the garage."

"There you go. That's when I started imagining you."

~ February, 2014

Dragged to heaven

HE IS ROBBED—stabbed—and death begins
dragging him up the wall, leaving
a streak. At the top of the wall his head
catches in razor wire—but death wrestles
it loose and drags him whole, spirit and
flesh, all of it, up and into the hot night.

There is rarely time to bury the bodies
now, and even then they are dragged
from the ground eventually, a coffin open
or falling out of the sky behind them.

~ September, 2013

Dinosaur

ER ASSISTANTS were brushing bones inside a low fence marked by a string. I was staring at the skeleton. "It's big," I heard myself say. I felt like a child saying that. The cave arched like a cathedral above us, dotted with stalactites—we were high in the mountains, finally at the dig site after days of travel.

The archeologist nodded. "Big, yes. But descended from a bird-hipped plant eater—about the size of a robin." She made a fist and wagged it at me, smiling—her eyes glittered, pretty behind dusty glasses.

I traced the shape of the dinosaur's arm, sunken in rock, which stretched almost twenty feet across the floor, then bent at the elbow and ran up the wall like a twisted beam, finally breaking into a jigsaw of finger bones.

"Where's its head?" I asked, trying to orient myself.

"It rolled into the river."

I didn't see a river, but the archeologist patted my shoulder and pointed, "There. See? The smooth rocks? There was a river here. Water carried the head into the bedroom."

The archeologist's assistants had named the next part of the cave "the bedroom." The bed was a large rectangular slab of granite that jutted from the back wall. A low ceiling muffled our footsteps as we approached the dinosaur's skull. It rested against the foot of the bed, as big as a van, egg-shaped, cracked, its jawbone shattered in pieces on the floor.

"Here's what I want to show you." The archeologist pulled a small flashlight from her vest and shined light through a hole behind the ear. "Have a look."

As I shimmied in, dust from her hair filled my nose—she needed a bath. The inside of the skull was scoured clean. After a moment I shook my head. "What am I looking for?"

"See how large the cavity is?" She watched my eyes, waiting. "The brain must have been enormous—more than a ton of mass."

It took a while for that to sink in, but I frowned. "The brain to body ratio must be small." The T-Rex brain, I knew, was bigger than a human brain, but cognition was limited; most of its functions managed the complex movements of a large body. "Have you calculated the ratio for this dinosaur?"

"It is about the same as ours."

"Are you sure? So it could think as clearly as a human?"

"We think so, yes."

I looked around the room with a new sense of awareness. There were two large granite blocks in the corner of the room and I laughed.

"I know, I know. Bedside tables." The archeologist grinned, showing me the two crooked teeth under her nose. "Let me show you the study."

We lowered ourselves over a series of platforms by the entrance to the cave, which I now recognized as a staircase. When we reached the bottom I brushed myself off and the archeologist patted pockets for her glasses. The study was larger than the bedroom. Sunlight poured from a slanted tunnel in the ceiling, and from a wide hole in the western wall.

The archeologist gestured towards the hole. "We found various items scattered by the window there. We've also found bones in this room that belong to an Eoraptor—a dog sized meat-eater more commonly found in Argentina. And of course the dinosaur's desk. It's over here."

The dinosaur's desk. It was shaped like a school boy's desk but loomed above us, chiseled from stone, roughly the size of a one story house—two drawers on the right supported a flat platform with room underneath for a huge chair. It was littered round by what looked like very large pencils; the tips were black stone, igneous, perhaps for carving.

"Our pickup truck was able to drag open that lower desk drawer—we attached a chain to the handle. Inside we found a stone tablet. It's over here."

The tablet was etched with a series of symbols and letter forms arranged in five clear lines. A thought began to trouble me. "Are you sure this was a dinosaur?"

The archeologist studied me cautiously and touched her glasses before answering. "The fossils fit nicely into the Theropod tree. It's spinal structure almost matches records of Therizinosaur. It's true there are some missing links in the evolutionary chain, but we'll find them."

"Okay, I'm just going to say it, because I feel like there's an elephant in the room. You know what that reminds me of?" I said, pointing at the stone tablet. "The ten commandments. Or five of them anyway."

The archeologist bit at her lower lip and sighed. "Yes, and?"

"What do you mean, *and?*"

"We don't think a dinosaur wrote the ten commandments."

"Maybe this wasn't a dinosaur!"

She looked at me incredulously. "God wrote the ten commandments."

I raised my eyebrows and stared at her significantly.

"So you think this dinosaur is God ... was God?" She asking, folding her arms.

"No, but—" It sounded ridiculous when she said it like that. "All I'm saying is ...." The archeologist's nostrils flared. She really was very pretty. I let it go and turned back to the desk. "Okay, what about the top drawer?"

She was happy to move on. "It seems to be stuck. We're setting off a series of small explosions around its base this afternoon."

I nodded and began pacing the room. "And the items here by the window?"

"Those are pieces of the chair—we think it was thrown. Here, possibly a leash for the Eoraptor. We found impressions in the clay that suggest the dinosaur wore pants."

"Pants? It wore pants?"

"Crudely sewn together. Some kind of leather hide, but yes, pants."

I was losing my ability to understand.

The archeologist continued. "We think it was confused. It seems to have lived a very long time—1,300 years according to our carbon dating team back at the university. And it lived alone, except for its dog ... uh, the Eoraptor."

I decided not to question the results of her carbon dating team. Instead I asked, "Why would it be confused?"

"Well, it's impossible for memories to persist much longer than two hundred years in a biological brain. Deterioration of memory protein patterns is well documented in Bowhead whales, for example, which can live two hundred years or longer."

"So this *dinosaur* wouldn't have remembered being born or growing up?"

The archeologist narrowed her eyes. "I guess that's true. Perhaps it thought of itself as having always existed. That's where you're going with this, right?"

"And there was only one?"

"There must have been more, but we've only found one." She looked at me suspiciously, waiting.

"Sounds like a lonely life," I said. I was tired. I wasn't going to bring up the whole dinosaur-God thing again, but it was depressing standing there in the middle of its bones. "I'm going to head back to my tent. You're welcome to join me later on, if you're up for it."

She laughed, hesitating just a moment to make up her mind. "Good, I've been saving a few beers. Are you sure you don't want to stick around while we blast that other drawer open?"

"No thanks. I already know what's in it. The other five."

"Yeah?" She said, tapping the dust off her glasses. "We'll see."

~ October, 2012

The god of empty air

THIS GOD'S ABSENCE is proof of him.
Our eyes see everything on all sides—
robes of folded nothing hang
behind the rain. Behind that, again,
nothing. We turn the blank pages of his book
and walk in all directions, not knowing where or
when to stop. He carries our voices
but not far. We die looking right at him.

~ July, 2013

One found dead

I WAS THE ONLY ONE who made it out.
The others? I didn't want to think about it. They were dead. My radio came to life with a report—huge numbers; the kind that don't mean anything. Billions. Did it matter? Just me left (one) and the announcer (two) explaining how it happened, so suddenly ... although it had been coming for some time—there were predictions, he said. If we had only *listened*. No one was left to search for bodies so nothing could be confirmed.

Then, suddenly, he reported survivors, eight or nine. How had they escaped? He asked. It really wasn't that bad, they answered, and they'd seen others. *Should we go back and help them?* An argument broke out, I couldn't tell who was talking, but then—the others were there too, on the radio. Someone said they looked okay—a long line of them—and why was everyone so upset? The announcer explained: the End. It came.

I was at my window. There was fog everywhere. He couldn't be sure, the announcer said, but the death toll was dropping. I saw a man in the street going about his business. Lights turned on in one of the towers and the cough of a motor starting broke the silence. There were several announcers now. They took turns. Facts were pouring in. They said they were relieved. Everywhere they looked they felt cautiously optimistic. The death toll—less than a million now, a thousand, only a hundred or so—and then they found the missing children in that school, locked together in the gym—until only one was left. Only one was unaccounted for.

~ May, 2013

Brontosaurus

HEAVY Camarasaurus suffers. Children stand in front of his bones and read the name on the plaque. It is not his name. He stares down at them—his mouth pried open—hating science.

~ October, 2012

Paleontologist Othniel Charles Marsh attached a Camarasaur's head to the body of an Apatosauruses and claimed he had discovered a new type of dinosaur called a "Brontosaurus"—to outdo his rival paleontologist Edward Dinker Cope during the "Dinosaur Wars" of 1877—1892. Although the Brontosaurus myth was debunked early in the 20th century, their skeletons still stand tall in Natural History museums across America.

What happened to Larry?

THERE WAS A COMPUTER in the back yard, behind our begonias; we could see it dragging the dog into the barn.

Mom went for the shotgun. "Where's your sister?"

"Still at school, remember? Soccer practice." I was whispering.

"Good. Jill's too old now. How old are you?"

"Mom. Really?"

"The spray paint is next to the door. Go! Before it gets into the stable."

Dad used to say *Computers are a funny kind of smart*, but this one didn't look very smart; I didn't understand what it was doing with Buck, but I don't think it did either.

"Hey." I was scared.

"Child." It pointed something at me. It was sort of wearing one of Buck's legs and it kicked itself across the straw. I sprayed blue paint over all the eyes as fast as I could.

This computer was pretty big. It had trash stuck on and packed in everywhere. I found a shopping bag in one of its hands; inside there was a candle, a badly sharpened pencil and some paper with drawings of the sun and hills.

"Did you get it?" Mom called. It sounded like she was in the garden.

"Yeah. I'm going to bury it."

"Give it some time. And get your sister to help. Cut all the wires with the scissors from the big drawer in the kitchen. Remember what happened to Larry."

~ July, 2011

40

The god of bears

THIS BLUE GOD eats bears to hide them
and hide from them. He looks like a tugboat
made of sacks full of small bears trying to escape
from the sacks, lazily. Do not feed this god. Do not
shoot this god with a gun. This god can hibernate
at will and is half dream—you cannot trick him
by falling asleep *or* waking up, you can only
trick him by dying. When you die
his fur arms surround you.

~ February, 2014

Bill and Mabel give birth

MABEL GAVE BIRTH to her daughter's head and arms—she pulled them gently from her mouth, gagging a little. Bill gave birth to her legs and hips through his single wet nostril. Once both halves of the child were wiggling in the crib, Bill and Mabel stood back, holding tall glasses of water.

"That was worth it," Mabel said after a while. She didn't really know if that was the right thing to say.

Bill looked over at Mabel and raised his huge eyebrow. "Was it?"

"Yeah. Now we have this baby."

Bill had no idea what Mabel was getting at. Maybe nothing. New parents were like that. He looked back at the two halves of their daughter, "I feel like this could be better," he said; he leaned over the crib and stuffed loose bits of their daughter back into her halves like he was stuffing two pillows. "Get some tape."

Mabel brought back some duct tape from the kitchen and helped Bill tape their daughter together around her mid-section; they put her on the floor and she started crawling in a circle, growling, trying to bite her tail.

"Hey," Mabel said. "She reminds me of someone."

"It's me," Bill said. He was thinking the same thing.

"No, not you. Maybe my dad. Or my mom. Maybe both of them. You know, stuck together."

~ March, 2013

42

The last person

A ND THEN the last person was dead.
Her heart stopped, sliding into its lock—
lungs and other organs unspooled—
the brain dark in its skull—
no electricity.
Finally.

◆

Finally the time had come. One by one, they climbed out of her. Two of them held her anus open while the others squirmed through, shielding their eyes; they had only seen the rosy glow of light through layers of skin—never like this, never warm on their own hands and faces.

They lashed ropes around their animals and hauled them out next, out the greasy tunnels—digging aside tangles of lymphatic vessels as the pack beasts emerged, bellowing, long-haired and clumsy. Some who'd been left behind cut at the thick dermis from the inside, clawed through it, and lay sprawled out, covered in plasma, exhausted. Smaller herding animals scrambled up after them, yapping and running in wide circles.

~ *March, 2013*

Garage sale

I FOUND THE LAST PARTS of God in a huge cardboard box at a garage sale. The gears were stuck and the leather seat was torn open. The woman wanted three dollars, but all I had was a buck twenty-five and that was fine with her.

I dumped the contents of the box in my front yard, next to my old Chevy up on blocks, and puzzled out how the triangular jaw fit onto the face, and then how the whole heavy head attached to the linked spine and the big black chains hanging down on either side. The gas tank was rusted through, so I went to the junk yard and found one that fit okay.

One of the neighborhood kids was messing around with the wheeled feet when I got back.

"This is dangerous," I told him. I had to hold his arm to get him to look at me. My kid on the other hand—I got him outside sanding rust off the frame.

"What's this thing for anyway?" He asked, folding his arms across his chest.

"Well, it made this whole world with you, me, and everything in it. So I guess it's for making worlds." He nodded and I gave him some nails to straighten.

It took a week for us to get it all bolted together and laid out. It looked like a huge half eaten fish. I attached a cable to each shoulder and winched it up, trying to get it standing—but I didn't want to go too far or it might fall on the house.

The mailman stopped to look at it.

"You're getting that old thing going again?"

"Yeah, almost there. Hopefully it's put together right."

"Well, good luck!"

It rained all night and I forgot to cover it with the tarp, so I had to wipe off the seats with a rag. But besides that it was ready to go. I got my son up in the driver's seat and towed the whole mess down the road to the high school, where we could drive it around on the soccer field without hitting anything.

"What are all these switches for, Dad?"

"I'm not sure. We'll have to try them out."

"You mean ... we're going to make a world?"

"Nope. God is." I winked at him and swung myself up into the passenger seat.

My son turned the key and it started up like a lawn mower on the third try—we didn't even need the jumper cables.

Forward and backward were pretty easy. It took a little longer to find pitch and yawl. "Try pushing on the whole steering wheel," I told him. Okay, that was how we kneeled, and pulling back on the wheel stood us up again. I stuck my head out the window and looked down at the shifting folds of metal. What did it look like? Honestly, you had to use your imagination to make it look like anything.

"This is awesome!" My son yelled over the noise of the motors. The levers on the first tray were for digging, drilling, and raking—they controlled a kind of chisel plow, a small rotating spike, and an uneven disk harrow. The valve on the dash controlled the flow of water through an array of nozzles that sprayed a cloudy mist in every direction. Next to that were the controls for an air seeder and a seed drill.

We made a series of small hills, dug a pond, and planted some trees. Before long the red light of dusk filled the cabin.

My son frowned. "This is going to take forever!"

I flipped to the beginning of a manual I'd found in the glove compartment. "It says here it takes seven days."

"Wouldn't it have been a tiny world then?" He looked confused. "I wonder who made the rest of it."

I didn't want to admit it, but he was right. I looked at my son, glowing in his seat. "I guess we must have."

~ July, 2013

Radios, 1956

THE RADIO PANTED up the stairwell and shoved open the heavy metal door to the roof deck. Wind whistled against his antenna. Fifty stories below the city burst in every direction, glittering.

The radio turned up his volume and peered down at the pedestrians on 3rd Ave; they would never be able to hear from so far away.

His voice was full of trumpets and cymbals, and then the light twittering of a female announcer. Where were the other radios? It didn't matter. He would sing anyway—with a sudden baritone—to that television on 83rd Street high up in her window. Sometimes TVs got nervous ... and sure enough, exasperated, she mouthed back a message, which jumped from actor to actor's lips as her channels changed: "*Not yet*—Can't you tell?—They're—watching me!"

~ January, 2013

Fairy tale

SHE HADN'T asked for this—to be in his dreams so often. But here she was, again. The boy gathered himself into a cloudy omnipresent mass of REM as Jill sat on a log and brushed off her skirt.

"What next, Chief?" Would he chase her through the forest? Would that annoying bear run her down? Ever since his father returned, the boy's dreams had been unpleasant. Jill just didn't like being pushed around.

"I'm lost." The boy said. He converged above her, floating in a pool of light.

"No you're not," she told him. "You're dreaming." She watched him struggle with that, wringing his hands. "It's okay, you won't feel lost when you wake up."

"I don't want to wake up."

"Too bad. You have to." She knew it was what he wanted to hear—that he had no choice. She'd tried to be nice to him before.

He stared at her. "I recognize you."

"You dreamed about me twice this week already. You must like me."

"No. I don't like you!"

This was heading south quickly. Jill kept her eye on the bushes.

"I feel scared. Is something bad about to happen?"

"Nothing bad is going to happen, okay? It's just you and me in here, kiddo. Nothing to be scared of."

"What about bears?"

"What about your dad? Lets talk about your dad."

He grinned at her. "There's a bear behind you."

It was too late this time. But next time—next time she was NOT going to put up with this bear crap; she didn't care what the bear "represented" in the boy's subconscious, she was just going to kill the fucking thing. It would be easy once she had control—a snap of her fingers, she thought. And then the lights dimmed and she felt herself being torn into smaller and smaller pieces of paper.

~ April, 2013

Widow's Vision

Imagined as a additional chapter to be inserted on page 73 of Oliver Sacks' book "Hallucinations."

UNLIKE CHARLES BRONSON SYNDROM—Widow's Vision (WV) patients suffer hallucinations that are subtractive; that is, the occipital cortex selectively removes real objects from the field of vision, instead of adding imagined ones.

Some argue that WV hallucinations are not entirely subtractive because the empty "space" left by a negative hallucination is filled with impressions supplied by the inferotemporal cortex. For example, if a bear attacks a WV patient—lets call her Mary—Mary's mind may remove the bear from her field of vision (and in acute cases, she will not hear the bear, smell it, or even feel it attacking her) and replace it with an unremarkable woodland scene, a backdrop cobbled together from a primal lexicon of forest imagery based on whatever *posteriori* experiences usefully match the environment.

Although this bear-attack scenario may seem juvenile, it does serve to illustrate the second primary aspect of WV, that is: the determining mechanism by which objects are removed. Typically a subject has no direct control over the targets of WV's subtractions (sometimes called "erasures" in the literature)—rather, a patient's mind subtracts exactly the objects they wish to focus on the most (i.e., an attacking bear). For this reason, WV is sometimes referred to as *La Vision Périphérique*.

In a letter Mary describes being tucked in by her mother as a child:

I would hear the door open, and feel the curtains billowing beside my bed. Mother would sigh into her rocking chair and turn the pages of Slovenly Peter or Peter Rabbit, reading quietly—this woman I had never seen. If I forgot myself and turned to ask a question, she would be gone. No more bedtime story, no more mother. If I was stubborn and scrambled out of bed to look for her, any evidence that she ever existed would vanish. The rocking chair, the books, until finally I would be left standing in an empty room. So I learned to let my mother creep up on me. Only then could I sense her in the room with me—see the blue of her dress from the corner of my eye, or hear her voice—barely more distinct than a memory.

Although Mary learned to outmaneuver her disability to some degree, she cannot sustain meaningful conversations with close friends or family even as an adult—as soon as she becomes too interested or engaged, they are erased from her sensory field. She has only ever seen the faces of strangers closely.

Of course Mary will never drive, enjoy a movie, a sunset, or look into a lover's eyes. WV is a type of sighted blindness. There is only "scenery," as Mary puts it, and the awareness of an emptiness rushing ahead of her, devouring, smoothing-over, guiding Mary through a life without trauma, rapture, or event. Mary is fond of saying, "I am married to this life but I have always been a widow."

~ May, 2013

Kites

SHE FLEW A KITE and we climbed up the string
together

and rested for a while kissing in the diamond shade.
From that height

I tugged the next kite from my backpack, fed
it into the sky and

we climbed on, but she fell into the ocean so I

was left alone. I climbed again, up
several more kites, a beanstalk of kites, until
I had gone all the way around the sky and found myself

back on the ground where I started. She

met me there dripping wet and so angry—she
just would not stop dripping.

~ February, 2013

Card trick

Sunday school had been canceled—it was Allen's first time in a chapel pew with his family. "Where's God?" He asked, already bored.

"Not so loud," his father whispered. "You have to be quiet."

They stared at the backs of a very tall blond family.

"He's over there." Allen's older brother said, motioning.

A large decorated rug draped over an animal of some kind was attached to one of the columns near the pulpit. A priest stroked the rug with an ornate brush as he read the gospel.

"That's God?" Allen whispered.

"Yeah, he's under the rug. That's his favorite rug."

"Zip it up you two," Allen's mother said.

There was definitely something under the rug. Allen could see it shifting its weight and breathing—dirty claws gripped the column.

A group of older women rang chorus bells at the alter.

"They're about to pass the collection plate, get out a quarter or something."

There was nothing in Allen's pocket except a deck of cards. He showed it to his brother.

"Not good. You don't have anything else?"

"I can do a card trick," Allen smiled.

There was a sound of splintering wood and distressed snorting—the animal slid down the column a bit and let go, hovering uneasily like a helicopter. After a moment it began paddling through the open spaces of the church with several furry paws. A quantity of brown liquid and debris dropped from beneath the rug and sloshed in the aisle. An alter boy put his hand on a mop at the front of the room.

"Gross—it stinks!"

"Who said that?" The voice seemed to come from everywhere and nowhere.

Allen's father turned to him. "Did you say something?"

"No. It wasn't me. I don't even smell anything."

"I didn't either, can't smell," Allen's brother chimed in.

"Well, somebody said it," the voice boomed out again.

There was silence now. The chorus bells had stopped ringing.

"Whatever …." The rug covered animal continued paddling down, then settled, lazily treading air in front of Allen. "Show me the trick."

Allen sat frozen on the pew. His brother jabbed him in the side. "Come on. Do what God says," he whispered.

Allen stood up, shrugged, and shuffled the deck between his hands dramatically, slapping it together with an exaggerated flourish. Everyone in the church was gaping at him; Mrs. Peterson, Allen's math teacher, looked especially horrified. "Pick a card, any card," he said. The animal pointed with a long claw. "Not that card," Allen said. "Any card except that card."

The animal thought for a while, then picked another card.

"Can you tell me which card you chose?" Allen asked.

"The six of spades."

"No no," said Allen. "You're supposed to say you don't know."

"But I do know."

"God knows everything," someone whispered helpfully.

"Nobody knows everything," Allen said.

Allen's father spoke up. "I'm so sorry everybody, it's his first time in church." He turned to Allen and ruffled his hair. "God does, Allen. It's true, God knows everything."

Allen flipped over the card in his hand, studied it for a while, then held it up. It was the five of diamonds. "The five of diamonds." Allen said loudly. "Not the six of spades."

There was general silence, then a low murmuring all around that gradually grew louder.

"It doesn't matter—it's just a stupid *card trick!*" Someone yelled.

"I think we should leave." Allen's mother grabbed his arm and before he knew it,

Allen was whisked out of the church and into his family's station wagon.

"I'm not sure we can go back there," Allen's father said as they pulled out onto the highway.

"I'm not sure we should, dear," Allen's mother said. "God got the card wrong."

Allen's brother was grinning at him from the other side of the back seat. "Good card trick," he whispered, then gave Allen a thumbs-up for the first time ever. Allen smiled back, nonchalantly slipping the six of spades from his sleeve and shuffling it back into his deck of cards.

~ August, 2008

Tooth troll

YOU COME OVER every morning, sweater
pockets full of teeth and we shake
them out onto the dining room table—
baby teeth, some rotted through, some heavy
with fillings or square as scrabble tiles:
dental glyphs slipped from a letterpress
of jaw bone, printing in the language
of sleep. You brought me a round plum
tooth (we held it up to the light), a pear-
sized tooth the next day and we dragged
bags of them onto the deck, shoveled the
smaller ones into piles and raked them
along the path like monstrous pearls.
Be quiet and watch me, you said when
I went with you one night. *They come out
so easily—the dream teeth—it's just like
picking berries!* And in the dark we ran
across backyards, squeezed under fences.
*Seize their secret language, the prize
of the dark other-mind, each word a rooted
shame—or wish—sweet, alive itself, all ours!*

~ November, 2012

Bones

DESPERATION DRIVES us to it. In the end, we all agree to build the machines—to find out what is left beneath us.

Iron claws peel back crust of the earth, setting aside its layers like ruined stacks of books.

Several days deep we hit a flat cellar of smooth matter. We scratch at it—bone. Our radar plots its gradual curve down and away on two sides ... a wide cylinder, roughly twenty miles in circumference.

We trace this bone like a fault line down the East Coast from Nova Scotia to Massachusetts—to what appears to be a finger joint, as wide as Springfield. Another bone, larger than the first, arcs off towards the Atlantic where we follow it under strata, a tectonic plate, finally into the dense mantle.

The whole fossil, some predict, must be larger than a continent ... although some believe it is no fossil—that our machines dig through the body of a living creature.

~ *July, 2013*

The graveyard where the dead go to bury their dead

THERE IS ANOTHER GRAVEYARD in the corner of the graveyard. One of the dead assembled there opens and closes his mouth.

With ragged hands in daylight they can still count and, although it took them all day to be sure, a woman is missing. They remember nothing about her, only that she belongs in this new hole and is dead, again. There are no loved ones now—no one will visit this second grave.

The dead are always out of breath and walk as slowly as shadows around a sundial. But there is still work to do: arranging branches on a tree as it grows, pushing aside fog to let a little light through, or digging these second, final graves.

~ August, 2012

God's wife

She strolls on Earth in the afternoon, her dress of trees
windy, hair just branches and brambles she ties
back with vines to see where she is placing bare
feet—on the sides of mountains, in soft marshes,
her body full of stones that crack and grind together
as she moves, becoming polished in her knees.

At night her earrings cast a million shadows
on the sheets as she makes their wedding bed—that old bed
shot through with asteroids, black at the foot from the
soot of moons and lopsided planets burned in their fireplace.
And then—there He is. Even with the universe expanding
she is crowded out by his bearish presence in the doorway
light years away. She shines like a moon for him as he roars—
tectonic shelves of his chest rearing up in front of her—
and when she looks down the length of him he disappears
into the distance. Somewhere far away, in some
other galaxy, he is entering her. Her hands settle on his
mane of endless, endless horses. He must be tired, this god
of hers. She is so very tired of him.

~ September, 2013

The dead machine

THE MACHINE FELL to its knees—the heat was too much—then twisted onto its side and powered down in the dust. The other machines formed a circle around it, but there was nothing they could do. The smallest of them reached down, unscrewed a chest plate and pulled out the dead machine's heart, which was still alive. They all watched as the heart squinted its eyes at the sun. It clung to the small machine's finger with two pink arms, shivering—a loose appendage flapping between its legs. The small machine lowered it to the desert and they all stood back. After a moment, the heart rose to its feet and started backing away from them, then turned and stumbled haltingly towards the mountains.

~ September, 2012

The yacht burns

PROBABLY VANDALS—poured gas on the deck. It sinks, engulfed in flames, on the 10 O'Clock news. The Police can't find the owner and there are no bodies, damaged property only.

We wait a month, no one claims the yacht. There is similar story on the news: a pickup on I-95 swerves into a tunnel wall. Horrific, twisted burning metal, but no one dead, doors jammed shut. *There must have been a driver. Yes, yes, he must have rolled away.* The license plate, blackened but legible, is registered to no one.

A house burns. "I don't know who lived there. Maybe nobody." A woman glares at the camera. "Why you asking me?" Anchors betray frustration. "Doesn't anybody know?" More houses burn, a school, a church. No one used them, officials say. Are there less of us than we imagined?

A small town in Nebraska burns. Drought. Unpopulated. Hikers find a burning abandoned country. Every tree and rock is on fire. We find a dark yellow dog. Its fur smokes when we shake it, a gorgeous dog. Children gather round, ready to cry but don't recognize it. "Whose dog is this?" A mother asks, angry, out of the blue.

Then one day we find a boy smoldering in a field with no family, no one knows him, even though we search for days. Soon there are more bodies—for a time they are everywhere—but for all practical purposes, our lives continue.

But there used to be more of us, right? We feel like there used to be more. We feel like we couldn't have built and burned all of this on our own.

~ November, 2012

Wives

Barney rummages through the cutlery
drawer until he finds his wife, under
a fork. He holds her legs and stirs.

Tiny white wife in a basket hanging
by her fingers from the clothes line,
it's a sunny day.

Folded in half, a wife eases
into an envelope like it's a tub—
she licks the stamp herself.

A wife drifting in her dress—
we watch her from business class
blowing out over marshland.

Chimney sweeps shoo them
from rooftops—their hems flap, they fall
past fire escapes.

The weather and mail and milk and door
men, they all take notice,
although Fred

lifts up the newspaper, glances
across the room and discovers that his
has been gone for years.

Finally the letters arrive, fanned
into our mailboxes. They all say
the same thing—*I'm safe*

and flying and I sleep so deeply now
stay away stay away stay away.

~ August, 2012

The god of art

IT DRAGS US by our hair to the sandbox and says, "Play."
We drag it by its hair to the office and say, "Work."

It runs, growing and growling, shedding limbs, tripping
on them, lifting away on wings that melt or snap,
inflating, leaving its skin behind, leaving its dying
body behind (we are the dying body).

This god is made of honey with the bees
still in it, and wishes—but greedy wishes!
This god is on a mountain pissing into the
mouth of North. This god sits in your
shopping cart and explodes. This god can't sleep.
This god vibrates in the bottom of a lake inside
your lungs—it flies itself like a kite and lets go
of the string. We burn it, we burn it, we burn it.

We trust it.

It lays us gently on the beach and stands barefoot
on our chests. It can answer all of our questions
but takes a long time. Its face is full of wind

when it talks and it's hard to UNDERSTAND ANYTHING
IN THE ROAR. Finally we grab its fat tail, but—
too late. It blows out our abilities like a candle.
It blows out our lives like a wolf.

It was there in the room when we were born.
When we died, it swam away unsatisfied.

~ November, 2011

Men

MOTHER AND DAUGHTER rode horses west under starlight. Mother had taken several drinks at the tavern and told stories with a loose tongue. "Listen, Daughter—I will tell you something else. Long ago horses had four legs. Many animals had four legs."

Daughter laughed and caught her mother's eye, but she was not joking.

"Do you see Sam's strong arms hanging by his sides? A thousand years ago, he'd have a pair of legs there instead. You would ride on Sam's back, not his shoulders—with the harness and saddle strapped here and here, like this." Mother patted her horse on his broad chest. "And his face would stretch forward under black eyes."

Daughter stared down at Sam, frowning, then pushed her hands through his curly blond hair and ruffled it. "What about Mike?"

"Yes, your little cat Michael too. He'd run around without any arms—just four legs and a head covered in fur, much less handsome. He wouldn't look anything like us."

"I can't imagine it," Daughter shivered.

"Many things were different then. The whales that crawl our southern beaches had no arms or legs at all—just one large paddle. They didn't walk on land and it was safe to live near the ocean."

"How could you know these things, Mother?"

They had reached a clearing and a cold wind blew the grass. "We will camp here tonight. Tie up Sam and Josh by the river. The woods beyond shelter lions—some so beautiful you may go to them willingly." Mother dismounted her horse and looked up at his body, steaming in the darkness. "It is time, Daughter, that you learned about men."

~ July, 2011

How I met Jorge

I N OLD SAN JUAN children and lovers fly kites on the wide yard in front of the Castillo San Felipe del Morro army base; at sunset their laughing shadows run in all directions.

One afternoon I took a hike along the shore. There is a brick path for tourists; it led nowhere, eventually ending at a windy outcropping of rocks. Other hikers chased hats down to the shore and it was fun to watch them float off into the sea. I also noticed a loose string, and idly traced it zigzagging down to the water, where it angled sharply into the sky. Someone must have lost their kite, I thought, and there was its string, tangled and anchored in the rocks. I squinted up, searching for the kite. Finally I saw it—a tiny dot way out over the bay—two, maybe three miles distant; it was almost inconceivable that someone could have flown a kite with such a long string.

I didn't have anywhere to be, so I took off my shoes and padded down toward the ocean. I wanted to hold that string. I wanted to fly a kite that was two miles away—a kite that you could barely see. It would be like flying an airplane.

The ocean swelled, lopsided, collapsing to fill gaps between the boulders—I jumped down and quickly wrapped the kite string around a strong stick. It was as tight as a piano string and pulled me toward the sea. Hard. But I managed to scramble onto a dry rock before the next wave rolled in.

Wind throttled the kite far above. The string hummed. A few families walked past, then a man in his mid twenties stopped.

"What are you doing?"

"I'm flying a kite that someone lost. I found the string in the rocks."

He looked at some of the loose string still tangled in the boulders, then up at the sky. "I don't see it."

I offered him the stick.

"Woah!" He staggered, then braced himself. A grin spread across his face. "This is amazing."

I laughed.

"My name is Jorge," he said after a little while. I couldn't tell if he was a local or visiting from another part of the country.

"I'm Raphe."

"We should pull it down."

It was a great idea—like reeling in a strong fish. "Okay, we can take turns."

A mixed crowd began to gather as we pulled lengths out of the sky—onto a growing pile of string at our feet—for the next hour. I was exhausted and took a break while Jorge worked at it on his own. Someone tapped me on the shoulder—a Chinese tourist—and offered her binoculars.

The kite danced as I played with the focus—still tiny, even through the binoculars. It wasn't in good shape. Two strips had torn off the body, flapping violently at its sides—and its short ribbon hung down, split in half and tangled in the frame. But as I stared I began to realize something. It wasn't a kite. It was Bugs Bunny. Bugs Bunny—or maybe Batman—from the Macy's Thanksgiving Day parade—or at least a parade balloon of some kind, partially deflated. Those were arms flapping at its sides, and legs swinging underneath—and a tiny head pinned to the top, shaking back and forth.

"It's still pretty far away," I told Jorge. "I think it's a balloon." I told him about the Macy's Day parade.

"There are no parades like that in San Juan."

I stared at him, frowning, then looked through the binoculars again. "Lets keep pulling."

"Mister, mister! Hey mister." A boy waved to me from the rocks. He was holding up a blue kite. I couldn't figure out what he wanted. I shook my head at him and focused on the balloon. Reeling it in got easier, and Jorge and I were able to pull faster as it edged closer to the ocean, away from the strongest wind.

The boy tugged on my arm. "Mister," he said. "I followed the string in the rocks. To the other end. It's attached to this kite. Look!" He held up the blue kite again.

Hold on, I thought—if the kite was at *that* end of the string, then what were we pulling down from the sky?

"It's a woman," Jorge said. He had the binoculars. "You're flying a woman."

"This is her kite," the boy realized, looking sadly at the blue kite in his hands. "It's a good kite."

I stopped reeling. There wasn't much resistance now—I could hold the stick with one hand.

Jorge looked at me and nodded. "If we pull her any closer the wind won't be strong enough to hold her up and she will fall into the ocean."

The waves chopped alarmingly. None of us would be able to swim out to help her.

Jorge asked a German tourist to call the Coast Guard. Ten minutes later a yellow boat motored around the jetty and began circling.

"Okay, lets pull her down," I said.

"Can I do it?" The boy asked.

Jorge looked at me and I shrugged. I handed the boy the stick and he expertly reeled in the woman. After a moment, the kite string sagged, then went slack—and we all—everyone in the now sizable crowd—watched the woman lean back and begin to fall away from the sky, slowly at first, end over end, then fast, head first, straight down like a pelican. She crashed into the side of a wave about fifty yards out. The Coast Guard motored over and a diver retrieved her from the water. We watched the boat in silence. Finally, with the help of the diver, the woman wobbled to her feet and waved at us, smiling weakly. The diver gave a thumbs-up.

The crowd erupted in cheers and the boy jumped up on a rock, tossing his arms back and forth. "Can I keep your kite?" He yelled. The woman nodded and the boy whooped and ran down the path, flying the blue kite behind him. Jorge slapped me on the back.

"Want to grab some food?" I asked Jorge after the excitement had died down.

"There's a good taco truck near the fountain."

"Perfect."

So that's how I met Jorge. We've been friends ever since.

~ April, 2014

68

I swim too far out

SHE SWIMS up my arm
I hear her

bells splashing

I pull her lips
over me like a dress
and light a match

What's wrong
the school
chorus
whispers

underwater
I'm drowning with my ex that's what's wrong what did you think was wrong

Follow our
tails

into a bath
of dirty water

She is in a light

bulb
on fire
like a filament

I swim after her toy whatever
she wants
far into the ocean

my mother watches the riptide
work
pacing the shore

sure I will die

*

There are planets in the ocean

half-buried in sand

and comets that sink
like necklaces

I find the planet Death

There's life down there
man-made structures

Walls, roads
Dead relations float up like bubbles
to tuck me in

I wish
explosively
from my face

that my bedroom light will turn on

and it does
She's standing on the bed

I glimpse her fins through fabric
a shimmering
underneath

She looks down
from both sides of her head

Fish with the mind of a fish

what are you thinking?

A foghorn blows
all my hair off

~ March, 2014

Harvest

THE SMALLER DEVILS are gamey. I brush them with
mint jelly and pull off their legs while my sister arranges
more in rows on the grill. We spit their teeth onto a little
tin plate—they can be used as tacks. On dull afternoons
like this we retire into the shade and scrimshaw
wishes on their horns. There are many types of devils
tanning in our lowlands. Lured by flesh, they creep
through the grass—tough as boot leather, slow to die.
They carry no trident, as stories tell, but their spines
fork and, once removed and dried, make elegant cutlery.

We catch angels like spiders would, in webbed nets, strung
between our satellites; machinery lowers them through
the clouds onto the ship. Sometimes an angel's belly
is swollen. When the healer cuts it open there is a gush
of freezing water from the vacuum as stars clatter
onto the deck—each the size of a charcoal brick.
Today we've caught only one, but she is enormous.
We lay her on the beach at low tide, free her
robe with scythes, and begin sewing it into a bright
new sail. Her belt will draw our anchor. Hooked
knives are pulled like garden hoes to slough the skin

in strips; we fire the mighty tryworks and boil the bible leaves.
Next, the mason's boy is lowered into her mind to ladle
precious oil with his bucket—hundreds of gallons. It takes
days of work without sleep. When all is done, we hang
her shining halo on our hall, wreathed round with feathers.

It takes three tribes to hunt a god. If one touches down
inland, we drive it through old cities with masks until
it falters, exhausted, dragging a tangled cape of cables and
raod signs, stumbling through rusted cars along
the avenues. We disorient it with spray-painted decalogue
and herd it towards a river where our kill ships wait.
It usually ends in shallow water. We build a scaffold
to mount the monstrous remains; our drills bore down
towards its heart—sometimes for days—until the black
liquid bubbles up and we hear the sigh of the universe
all around us. Four men on a crosscut saw through the fingers
and count growth rings while a shaman works his way
into the belly, searching for nourishing roots that grow there.
Once, years ago, men and women cut off the head and arms
and set great oars through the ribs to try and row their way
to heaven. Today we set the picked carcass ablaze
and float it at the horizon, a gift to luck.

~ August, 2012

Joey's closet

"There's something in the closet."
"Did it hurt you?"
Joey shook his head.
"But you're scared of it? Why are you scared, buddy?"
"Well. It came in here and LOOKED AT ME and then it was FLYING AROUND and then it grabbed me LIKE THIS and we went into OUTER SPACE and it was REALLY REALLY SO FAST and it had BIG EYES, and then it killed a SPIDER!"
"But that sounds like fun."
"No. *It's not fun.*"

"Whatever's in his closet is taking him into outer space," I said.
Jill looked concerned, but kept scrubbing. We were both exhausted. Joey had been waking us up several times a night; this was the third week.
"Put a positive spin on it."
"I tried. It might also be taking him back in time. He drew those." I pointed with a dish rag to Joey's pictures of dinosaurs that I'd stuck to the fridge.
"Hey," Jill said. "Those are pretty good!"

I took a close look at Joey's closet. There were two extra copies of *The Hungry Hungry Caterpillar*, a diaper box with the last diaper still in it—that we'd never have to use, I realized with a twinge of sadness and relief—and lots of battery operated stuffed animals that had died. I checked the walls for hidden panels and poked at the ceiling with a broom. Nothing unusual. Standard closet. But I did find several clumps of long wiry white hairs.

"What are these, buddy?"

Joey pulled at my beard.

"The thing in your closet has a beard?"

"Yes, daddy. A BIG BIG one. And it was ON FIRE like a BIG TALKING BUSH."

"I think God is in his closet," I said to Jill.

She stared at me for a while. "That makes sense," she said, finally. "You could take him to church. To test your theory."

I wasn't gung-ho about that idea.

"He'll be fine." She smiled at me. "You'll be with him."

I buckled Joey into the car seat and pointed my GPS at the nearest church.

"Daddy? Where are we going?"

"Well, you know that thing in your closet?"

"*The bad thing.*"

"Yes, the bad thing. We're going to look for its home."

I thought he might throw a tantrum, but he didn't. Instead he said, "I'm going to tell it—go away from the closet!"

I laughed and ruffled his hair.

As we pulled into Saint Vincent's parking lot, I could see shadowy movements passing rapidly back and forth behind the stained glass windows. Joey saw them too—his body was trembling as I pulled him out of the car seat. I carried him up the stone path and then dropped him onto his feet. He put his hand in mine.

The minister slipped out of the church to greet us. "Hi there! How're you folks doing today?" His hair was badly disheveled and he was out of breath.

"We're fine," I said. "Hard work?"

"Oh, well. It is what it is."

"Can we go in?"

"Of course, of course. We're all God's children." He lead us into the church and seated us in the last row. "You might want to stay back here for a little while," He said, then ran down the aisle, his black robe flying behind him like a cape.

"Is that the thing in your closet?" I asked, pointing at God as he twirled between the rafters at the front of the church.

"*Yes.*" Joey whispered. He'd burrowed under my arm. "Why is that man chasing it?"

"Well, it's his job to get God's attention." We watched the minster sprint past the dias and crash into the baptismal font that God had dropped onto and was slurping water from. God exploded like a flock of birds, then galloped across a mural on the ceiling and down a column, leaving a black pattern of hoof prints. The minister crouched, then expertly hurdled one of the pews and caught a handful of God's beard as he passed—and they tumbled into the aisle together.

The minster waved; he'd straddled God's neck and was laughing, smoothing back and braiding God's hair as He rooted through a pile of hymnal books and old bibles, chewing up their pages.

I walked Joey up the aisle.

"Go ahead," I said.

Joey looked at God, then back at me.

I smiled at him. "It's okay, buddy. I'm right here."

Joey stepped closer; hair lifted off his head as God breathed in, smelling him.

"Please will you go away from my closet?" Joey asked God.

God snorted and looked down at Joey, then up at me; his eyes *were* huge—undulating amniotic sacks, full of jellyfish. One of the jellyfish dripped onto the floor.

"My wife and I need some sleep," I explained.

The minister tapped me on the shoulder. "He can't hear you."

"What? Why not?"

"You have to pray. He can't hear unless you pray."

I stared at the minister and realized that what he was telling me was true. I closed my eyes and took a deep breath. "Please, God," I began. But I stopped.

"So?" Jill asked. She looked really tired.

"He won't go away unless we pray to him."

"And what's the problem?"

I shook my head and grimaced.

"You stubborn! Selfish! Son of a ... sorry excuse for a .... What about me? I need to sleep or I'm going to die!" She yelled, looking around for more and more things to throw at me.

I peeked in on Jill and Joey from the hallway. They knelt by Joey's bed with bowed heads. The closet door was closed—smugly so, I thought. Maybe Jill was right, maybe I was being too stubborn. But, darnitall, this was Joey's room. And Joey was *my* son—he shouldn't have to be afraid of anything.

This was not over, I decided. Not by a long shot. Even if I had to fill that closet with concrete. Even if I had to fill up every closet in the whole damn town.

~ April, 2014

The Elephant Girl with three fathers

W E SAW HER on the F train first—a normal girl except for those huge elephant eyes hanging low in her cheeks, like plums. Anyone who wanted to be her father could join them, her three fathers said. Many greying men accepted. What else would they do with their lives?

People who thought they were little girls wanted to be her friend, but there are no such things as little girls so the Elephant Girl didn't want to be friends.

In the morning, she climbs out of tunnels onto the subway platform. Her grey fathers follow her, stumbling over the tracks. Late at night, she leads them out a sewer grate onto the shore by Battery Tunnel—they step onto the water, watching the Statue of Liberty glow, and lie on the waves to sleep.

One day a big man in a business suit pushed the Elephant Girl—right between her elephant eyes. He would not be her father. She pushed him back, and when she did that, he shrank to half his height. It happened over and over until he was gone.

Her fathers watched it all and solemnly sang the blues.

~ February, 2013

Cave god

He fell out of the ocean long ago—crawled on his soggy
hands here. Now it's ninety thousand B.C. and he lives in a cave
covered in coarse black hair.

At night he strikes rocks with other rocks, anticipating
what? He doesn't even know he is God—learning
slowly, evolving slowly.

He makes them in his image: the Cro-Magnon,
Neanderthal. They stumble disoriented into grasslands, dust
arms pulled into the sky by tails of wind—there is no Word to bond
the atoms, yet.

Some days he strays into the forest, seized by a compulsion to kill.
Usually he is torn apart by lions and lies on his back—
allowing himself the rest, to be broken—
watching dusk point at dawn—pink fingers of cloud extending across
the ceiling of their own enormous cave.

~ January, 2013

Vampires, Werewolves, Zombies

THERE ARE EVIL PEOPLE called Vampires who are born and decay in a very short period of time—only eighty years or so—while the rest of humanity is forced to suffer their jealousy. We identify Vampires by their stunted teeth, ruddy skin, physical weakness, and constant complaining. Some become so enraged by their disadvantages that they hammer wooden stakes into the hearts of our more dapper and distinguished citizens. In fact, the only way to defend yourself from a Vampire in one of its violent tantrums is to bite it on the neck and suck all its blood out. Although this may sound difficult, the task is made easier by seducing the Vampire beforehand; it becomes pliable and easy to puncture.

If Vampires weren't enough, there are Werewolves stalking our foggy woods and marshland. Once a month, during the full moon, they fill their pistols full of silver and run in packs through the woods, shaking torches, shooting their victims rudely in the heart. An insult worth retaliation, no doubt there—but Werewolves are exceedingly difficult to dispatch. If it is attempted, you must approach a pack quietly and pick them off one by one, first dragging them into the forest, then seizing one of their limbs in your mouth and vigorously shaking it back and forth until the Werewolf bleeds out. It is an unpleasant routine to be sure, but the only surefire way to deal with these foul creatures.

Of course, the most dreadful scourge are the Zombies, who don't care to discriminate; they'll use all manner of weapons—shovels, shotguns, hammers, knives, household furniture—towards one goal and one goal only: to forcibly remove your head from your body. Holding both arms out in front of you affords some degree of protection, but the only foolproof way to halt their mad obsession is to eat their whole body mouthful by mouthful. The following technique is especially effective: open their bellies by pressing down hard with your fingernails and scoop large amounts of intestine into your mouth. It should also be noted that moaning frightens Zombies into dropping their weapons—so try moaning, even while eating a Zombie.

~ February, 2013

Pulling the plug

Imagined as a additional chapter to be inserted on page 198 of Oliver Sacks' book "Hallucinations."

BECAUSE THE MIND apprehends music as a temporal whole and not as a static assemblage of pitch, timbre, and rhythm, it is easier to define the boundaries of musical hallucinations—as opposed to visual hallucinations—and so assume a certain degree of control over them.

In 1995 I received a phone call from Mary, an elderly patient of mine. Since her sixteenth birthday, Mary had "heard" *Good Night, Irene*—the 1933 version performed by Huddie Ledbetter—every evening before supper. The music was so loud that, often, Mary could barely understand her husband David when he spoke to her, even if he was sitting in the chair next to her.

Mary was calling to announce that the music had stopped.

Earlier on the day of the call, David got an idea. He located a copy of *Good Night, Irene* and cued it up on their CD player just as Mary's hallucination began. It took some fiddling but, with guidance from Mary, David was able to "line up" the music on the CD to the music in Mary's mind. Then they made a picnic of sandwiches and lemonade and sat back on the couch to enjoy the music together. After *Good night, Irene* had played ten or twenty times, David decided to turn in for the night and pressed "Stop" on the CD player. When he turned around Mary was holding her head. "It's gone!" She wailed. "The music is gone!" Mary's shock gave way to relief in the minutes that followed—which is when she called me to recount the startling experience. I monitored her over the following weeks and months. The music did not return. Indeed, she had been cured, and quite by accident.

I was able to administer David's "cure" to several other patients, aligning their auditory hallucinations with recordings of each source antagonist—effectively overlaying hallucination with reality—then abruptly stopping the cassette tape or CD. In most cases, the hallucinations also stopped.

I was inspired to attempt a similar experiment on patients who suffered recurrent or repeating *visual* hallucinations. This would be more difficult, I knew—I imagined I might even have to dress up and act like the subject of a hallucination. A friend of mine, an old stage actor, donated his repertoire of costumes and disguises. These remained stored in my wife's closet until an opportunity presented itself.

Jillian received daily visitations from her dead husband Jack and, over the years, I learned to plan my visits to coincide with his appearances, so as to monitor their interactions. As we spoke in her living room, Jillian would invariably tense and say, "Hold that thought, Dr. Sacks—Jack is at the door." After opening and closing her front door, she would return and excuse herself: "I know he's not really there, but if I don't let him in he'll just keep knocking." Usually Jack would sit silently at the dining room table, or watch the street from behind the front curtains. Jillian would look over her shoulder to check on him every few minutes.

One day Jillian produced a photograph of Jack. I immediately thought of my nephew—a striking resemblance—and contacted him that same afternoon. Here was the opportunity! My nephew hesitated but agreed to my scheme and I picked him up at the train station the following week. After a quick trip to the barber and a wardrobe change, we drove to Jillian's apartment. I instructed my nephew to wait outside and enter only once Jillian opened the front door. He was to then sit at the dining room table for a while, approach Jillian, explain that he could not visit anymore, and then leave. I hoped my nephew's exit would have the same effect as David pressing "Stop" on his CD player.

Jillian noted my anxiousness as we exchanged pleasantries—I wring my hands when I'm excited—but was soon distracted by Jack's "knocking" and stood to answer the door. What was about to happen? Would Jillian's mind conflate its visual hallucination of Jack with my real nephew as I hoped, or reject my nephew as a facsimile? Would Jillian see both Jack and my nephew waiting on the doorstep? Jillian took it in stride—she opened the door without fanfare, and returned to the couch. When I asked her where Jack was a few minutes later, she pointed casually to my nephew and said, "Over there at the table. His hair looks nice today." About twenty minutes later I gave the signal and my nephew approached us. Jillian nearly jumped out of her skin when he began speaking. "Jack is talking to me, Dr. Sacks! He's never said anything before!" Her distress intensified as my nephew explained that, although he enjoyed visiting her, this would be his last visit. When he opened the front door and left, Jillian ran to the window and watched him drive away. I pretended I hadn't seen anything and asked Jillian why she was upset. She said she needed to be alone—so I left, somewhat troubled myself.

Although the experiment was successful—Jillian's hallucinations did not return—she was understandably disconsolate during our following visit. She talked endlessly about Jack. She didn't understand why he had to leave, and was confused by the manner in which he left. How had he driven away in my car if he was only a hallucination? And how had I gotten my car back? I took the opportunity to explain the experiment. Jillian did not immediately appreciate my "presumptuous" intervention, but wrote me a letter the following month:

> I suppose you were right—I should move on. But if you had asked me to participate in your experiment, I would have refused and Jack would still be here. No ... that's not quite right. Jack is gone. The hallucination would be here. Either way, I feel obligated to write and say "thank you," although I am still angry.
>
> I also have one favor to ask. I wonder if you might provide me with the mailing address of your actor. I felt a kind of connection with him when he was here—perhaps he might even visit me one afternoon? I know that my feelings for Jack might complicate the matter, but I can't shake the notion that I should at least get in touch with your actor impostor. I don't even know his name!

Needless to say, I thought it unwise to provide Jillian with my nephew's mailing address or name. For his part, my nephew has commented on the experience several times, but only to express misgivings about the experiment in the context of a general concern for Jillian's wellbeing.

~ May, 2013

84

Bill and Mabel build God

BILL AND MABEL WENT to Catholic Company, which sells altars, six foot candles, incense, bibles, uncomfortable cushions—Mabel wanted to buy stained glass windows to smash in the parking lot behind their apartment. Instead she noticed, next to a balsa-wood nativity kit, a model-God kit. It included crazy glue and everything required to put Him together. The side of the box read, "For children of all ages." It was expensive but there was only one so Mabel bought it for Bill.

Bill loved the gift. He tore the box apart and spread out all the pieces on the rug so they could both help. Some of the parts were small and delicate—Mabel handled those pieces with her claws so Bill wouldn't damage them. And Bill read the instructions and helped hammer in the little nails and pegs with his hooves.

The instructions explained that, although the model kit wasn't *technically* a false idol, they should continue to direct prayers elsewhere—the sky was suggested as an alternative; moreover, it was repeatedly emphasized that the kit model was only a collectors item—not God Himself.

Still, it was hard not to think that maybe God was somehow *in* the model; the foot-tall figure was so lifelike, especially the severe marble eyes—and Mabel had done such a *good job* gluing on its sash, sandals, and cotton beard. What harm could come, really? It was too tempting to kneel down and ask it for things. They gave in.

If, later in Heaven, they were accused of some crime, Mabel planned to argue that their prayers were *intended* for Real God. It was just so much easier when there was something to look at—He of all people would understand that (Kit-God certainly would). And Bill was such a *visual* guy—for example, he could never follow directions. He always had to look at a map. Or, better yet, Google Earth. Bill only really understood when he was looking at Google Earth. Shouldn't it be as easy as that?

~ *February, 2014*

The devil fell on the gas station

THE DEVIL FELL through the clouds and landed on the gas station. I got there late and helped Brian sweep up the broken glass.

We joined a bunch of people who'd gathered to watch from the cemetery gate; the devil was galloping in circles, clapping his hands, raising quantities of dust. God stood on his hind legs—like a man—and let out a shrill whistle. Eventually they calmed down and sat in the high grass, staring at each other like cats.

~ August, 2008

Do not hunt the extinct animals

RAY AND HIS mother waved goodbye to their neighbors from the front porch—the Joneses slumped onto their lawn and burst into a cloud of dust, along with their luggage.

Ray's mother settled into a rocking chair, fiddling with her respirator. Its battery was almost dead. They all wore respirators now, even in the suburbs.

"I don't want to go," she said.

Almost everyone they knew had left—it wasn't just the Joneses. Ray sure as hell was leaving. A college student had posted instructions on the internet. Time travel. It was easy and it didn't cost anything.

"You have to go," Ray said. "It's no good here. If you stay I'll never see you again."

"Why? I don't understand why you can't come back, Ray."

"That's not how it works." Ray took off his respirator and held it out to his mother, but she waved it away. "If I try to come back, a new universe will split off—with a phony version of you—and carry me away with it." The scientists on TV had warned them. "You'll get lonely if you stay here. *No one* will come back."

Ray stared at the tattered American flag flapping against the mailbox. "We're going together, mom. We'll travel as a group, okay? Aunt Deb, her daughter Margo, Brian. Think about it. We can fix everything! Sink Christopher Columbus's ships, whatever it takes."

His mother grunted. "And how will you agree on what to do? I rather like Christopher Columbus."

It was true. Everyone had a different vision for a perfect world. Clean air, sure— but what else? Ray wanted to save the forests and the oceans—he wanted to see whales!

"Dad would go," Ray said.

She sighed. "I think you'll get lonely too, Ray. You won't be able to fix everything." She looked off towards the city and its halo of smog. "Not everything. And it's not so bad here."

Ray shook his head and went into the house for fresh batteries.

◆

It was 1873. A black dog with a headset chased a small dinosaur under the wheels of their covered wagon. *It's getting worse*, Ray thought. Ever since the whale. Yes, he had finally seen one ... being hoisted out of the ocean and into the payload of a hover craft.

Had the scientists seen *this* coming? People in every time period were learning how to time travel. It was so easy animals were figuring it out—Ray watched the small dinosaur unzip its atoms from their temporal plane, leaving a thin contrail of dust; the dog caught a mouthful, sneezed, and shook off its headset.

"I feel like time is getting all ... messed up!" Ray shouted over the rattling of the wagon wheels. "It's like the air back home. It's like time is ... " he struggled with the word reluctantly, "polluted."

"You crazy?" Brian yelled back. "Take a gulp of that fresh air! And anyway, you don't like it here? We can go wherever we want!"

But it was the same everywhere. They'd just come from the voter riots at the Bush-Gore election. Could citizens vote if they were from a different time? Benjamin Franklin thought so.

Ray's family had got off to a good start. They told Einstein about Hiroshima and taught oil tycoons how to farm wind. But then things got out of hand. Unpredictable. Like last week they passed an Assyrian king with a hundred white hunting tents squaring off against a bunch of environmentalists—they had staked up signs in front of buffalo that read, "Do not hunt the extinct animals." You couldn't tell what year it was anymore ... and if you asked, people didn't seem to care. Gangs of disillusioned "time immigrants" surfed the centuries like it was a big party.

Ray shielded his eyes from another nuclear explosion as two warring space ships detonated in the atmosphere off to the south, parts of their metal hulls glinting as they spun through clouds toward the mountains. Ray thought about his mother back home on her porch. He wondered who else had stayed behind. Couldn't have been many. A few cars on the highway. Nobody running the factories. Maybe the air was clearing.

~ October, 2012

No defense against the fish

THEY GIVE US pills so we forget the fish. They roll giant fish over our barricades, smashing men—we have no defense against the fish.

~ February, 2014

The highest roller coaster

EVENTUALLY THE AMUSEMENT PARK OWNERS were forced to face the facts. Gravity was not sufficient at such high altitudes to press roller coaster cars down onto the tracks or, for that matter, passengers to their seats.

The engineers of Splash Park's tour de force—untastefully christened "The Challenger"—believed they had taken all factors into consideration. They *hadn't* foreseen, however, certain riders' insistence on remaining suited in the spandex "space duds" obtained at rival Laser Tag Arena, which effectively lubricated passengers as they rapidly ascended, slipping through the troposphere and, unfortunately, out of the one-size-fits-all restraining harnesses.

The first child to reach escape velocity in this manner was never found—loud speakers on the park grounds repeatedly asked Billy to report to the front gates, where his father waited with his little brother, impatiently balancing an extra melting soft serve twist.

For a while, Coast Guard satellites kept an eye out, despite diagrams on the nightly news that convincingly demonstrated the boy's trajectory likely placed him far outside the known solar system.

~ May, 2013

About the author

Born in New Haven, Connecticut in 1979, Raphael Matto completed an MFA in Writing at Vermont College of Fine Arts in 2014 and now lives in Brooklyn, New York with his cat Milo. He aspires with all his heart to be an English Literature or Creative Writing teacher.